Gr 3-4

THE
CAMERA

Chris Oxlade

Heinemann Library

Chicago, Illinois

www.heinemannraintree.com
Visit our website to find out
more information about
Heinemann-Raintree books.

To order:
☎ Phone 888-454-2279
▭ Visit www.heinemannraintree.com
to browse our catalog and order online.

Edited by Louise Galpine and Laura Knowles
Designed by Philippa Jenkins
Original illustrations © Capstone Global Library Ltd 2011
Illustrated by KJA-artists.com
Picture research by Mica Brancic

Originated by Capstone Global Library Ltd
Printed and bound in China by CTPS

15 14 13 12 11
10 9 8 7 6 5 4 3 2 1

Library of Congress Cataloging-in-Publication Data
Oxlade, Chris.
   The camera / Chris Oxlade.
      p. cm. -- (Tales of invention)
   Includes bibliographical references and index.
   ISBN 978-1-4329-3828-4 (hc) -- ISBN 978-1-4329-
3835-2 (pb) 1. Cameras--History--Juvenile literature. 2.
Photography--History--Juvenile literature. I. Oxlade, Chris,
II. Title.
   TR149.09395 2011
   771.3--dc22
                                        2009049146

Acknowledgments
The author and publisher are grateful to the following
for permission to reproduce copyright material: Alamy
pp. **16** (© Mary Evans Picture Library), **22** (© Image
Register 007); Corbis pp. **4** (© Steve Prezant), **11** (©
Bettmann), **14** (© Bettmann), **17 bottom** (© Hulton-
Deutsch Collection), **21** (© Pulp Photography), **24**
(dpa); Getty Images pp. **7** (Hulton Archive/Apic) **8**
(Science & Society Picture Library), **10** (Science &
Society Picture Library), **13** (Science & Society Picture
Library), **15** (Science & Society Picture Library),
18 (Hulton Archive), **20** (Science & Society Picture
Library), **26** (Hulton Archive/Sam Shere), **17 top**
(Hulton Archive/Eadweard Muybridge); Photolibrary pp.
9 (Pixtal Images), **19** (North Wind Picture Archives), **23**
(Blend Images/JGI), **25** (Imagebroker.net/Anton Luhr),
27 (Alaskastock/Michael DeYoung); TopFoto p. **5** (The
Granger Collection, New York).

Cover photographs of a photo being taken on a digital
camera reproduced with permission of iStockphoto/
© Giorgio Fochesato and the world's largest camera at
Brighton Park, Chicago, Illinois, in 1900 reproduced
with permission of Corbis/© Bettmann.

We would like to thank Ian Graham for his invaluable
help in the preparation of this book.

Every effort has been made to contact copyright holders
of material reproduced in this book. Any omissions will
be rectified in subsequent printings if notice is given to
the publisher.

All the Internet addresses (URLs) given in this book
were valid at the time of going to press. However, due
to the dynamic nature of the Internet, some addresses
may have changed, or sites may have changed or
ceased to exist since publication. While the author
and publisher regret any inconvenience this may cause
readers, no responsibility for any such changes can be
accepted by either the author or the publisher.

CONTENTS

Look for these boxes

Biographies

These boxes tell you about the life of inventors, the dates when they lived, and their important discoveries.

Setbacks

Here we tell you about the experiments that didn't work, the failures, and the accidents.

EUREKA!

These boxes tell you about important events and discoveries, and what inspired them.

Any words appearing in the text in bold, **like this**, are explained in the glossary.

TIMELINE

2010—The timeline shows you when important discoveries and inventions were made.

BEFORE CAMERAS

Do you have a camera? What do you like to photograph? Photographers take photographs with cameras to record important events, create art, and to make advertisements. Before cameras were invented, people could only record what they saw by drawing.

The camera obscura

A **camera obscura** makes an **image** of a scene inside a box, but does not record it. For hundreds of years, artists used camera obscuras to help them draw. They placed paper under the image made by the camera obscura and traced over the image to copy the scene.

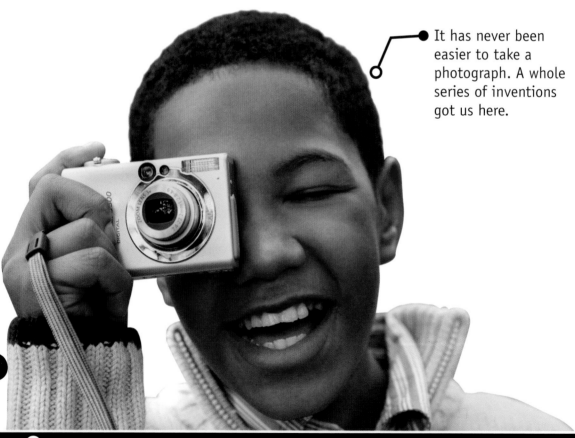

It has never been easier to take a photograph. A whole series of inventions got us here.

4

around 1000
—The camera obscura is invented

around 1300
—Eyeglass lenses are developed

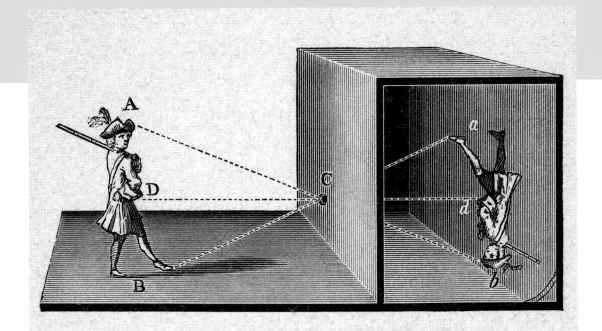

In a camera obscura, light from a scene passes through a tiny hole or **lens** in one side of a box, and an image of the scene is formed inside the box on the opposite side. Some camera obscuras were made up of whole rooms that the artist could stand inside. All camera obscuras collected light through a small hole until the 1500s, when eyeglass lenses were used to make the images much brighter and clearer.

This illustration from the early 1800s shows how a camera obscura works.

Canaletto (1697–1768)

Italian painter Giovanni Antonia Canal—known as Canaletto—is famous for his fantastically detailed paintings of the canals and buildings of Venice during the 1700s. One of Canaletto's most important tools was a camera obscura that he used to compose his paintings and drawings.

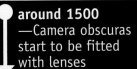

around 1500
—Camera obscuras start to be fitted with lenses

THE FIRST PHOTOGRAPHS

A simple camera is a lightproof box with a **lens** in the front. The lens bends light from a scene as it comes into the box, making an **image** of the scene in the back of the box. A photograph is a recording of this image. Recording an image was the biggest problem that the pioneers of photography had to overcome. They needed to find some sort of **light-sensitive** material to put in the back of a camera that would record the image.

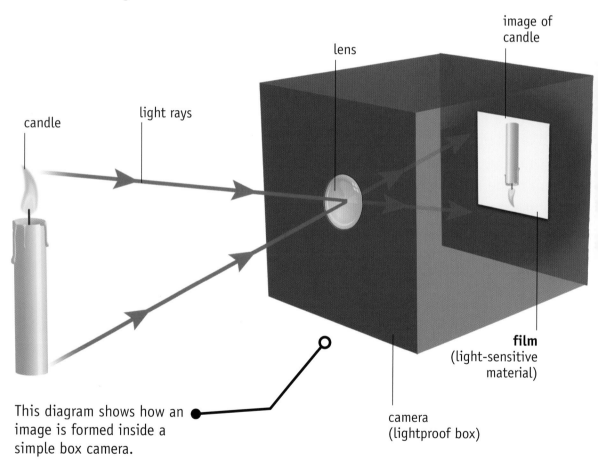

image of candle

lens

candle

light rays

film
(light-sensitive material)

camera
(lightproof box)

This diagram shows how an image is formed inside a simple box camera.

1816—Joseph Niépce records his first photographs

1824—Niépce tries using bitumen to record photographs

This is Niépce's first photograph, taken in 1827. It is of the view from the workroom window of his house in France.

Joseph Niépce *(1765–1833)*

French inventor Joseph Niépce was obsessed with the idea of photography and decided to try to record images formed by a **camera obscura**. In 1827 he took a photograph on a tin **plate** coated with **bitumen**. It is the oldest photograph that survives today. Only a year later, Niépce was taking high-quality photographs on silver plates. In 1829 he began working with Louis Daguerre (see page 9) to improve the photographic process.

Setbacks

Joseph Niépce tried all sorts of materials to record images, including acids spread on stone, but they did not react to light. Niépce gave up several times, but kept returning to the problem. In 1816 he finally recorded some images using chemicals called silver **salts** coated on paper, but these quickly disappeared in daylight.

7

1827—Niépce takes the first photograph that still survives today

1829— Niépce begins working with Louis Daguerre

1833—Niépce dies. Daguerre begins working with Niépce's son.

1834—The **zoetrope** shows moving images inside a spinning drum

1830

1835

The daguerreotype

In 1839 Frenchman Louis Daguerre had perfected a new photographic process. The photographs produced were called **daguerreotypes**.

Daguerre put a copper **plate** coated in silver into iodine **vapor** to make it **light-sensitive**. He put the plate in a camera and pointed the camera at a scene for several minutes. Then Daguerre held the plate in **mercury** vapor, which made the photograph appear. To prevent the photograph from being spoiled by daylight, it was bathed in salty water and dried.

Daguerreotypes quickly became all the rage in Europe and the United States. Portrait studios opened where people could have their daguerreotype taken.

EUREKA!

Daguerre discovered by accident that mercury made his photographs appear. He had put some partly exposed photographic plates in a cabinet full of chemicals. Later he was surprised to see **images** on the plates. By a process of elimination he found that mercury vapor had "**developed**" the plates.

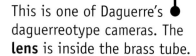

This is one of Daguerre's daguerreotype cameras. The **lens** is inside the brass tube.

8

Louis Daguerre *(1787–1851)*

Painter and designer Louis Daguerre was a **camera obscura** specialist. He met Joseph Niépce in Paris in 1829, and the pair worked together until Niépce's death in 1833. Daguerre then went into partnership with Niépce's son, Isidore, but made sure only his name was on the new process they invented. The rights to Daguerre's process were bought by the French government, which paid Daguerre a **pension** for the rest of his life.

1850s—Celluloid is invented

1851—Frederick Scott Archer invents the collodion process

Improving the process

After Louis Daguerre's success, the **daguerreotype** remained popular for more than 20 years. During this time, other pioneers gradually improved the process of taking photographs.

In 1840 William Fox Talbot invented a process known as the calotype. Photographs were taken on paper soaked in silver iodide **salts**. After being exposed in the camera, the paper was **developed** with chemicals to make a **negative image** appear. The negative could be used to make lots of positive prints.

In 1851 Frederick Scott Archer invented a process using silver salts dissolved in a syrupy material called collodion, which was spread on glass photographic **plates**. The process became known as the "wet-plate" process. In the 1870s Richard Maddox invented dry photographic plates, which were much more convenient to use.

This is a negative calotype image taken by William Fox Talbot in 1843.

1860s—Mathew Brady photographs the Civil War

Mathew Brady *(around 1825–1896)*

The Civil War (1861–65) was one of the first major events to be photographed. Mathew Brady was the most famous photographer of the war. During the 1840s, Brady had set up his own studio in New York City, where he became rich photographing the city's celebrities. When the Civil War started, Brady wanted to go and record it. But the life of a war photographer was not easy. The cameras, glass plates, and bottles of chemicals were heavy and difficult to carry. It was also expensive, and Brady lost most of his fortune during the war.

This photograph shows Mathew Brady (center) in front of his horse-drawn, photograph-developing wagon, during the Civil War.

11

1871—Richard Maddox invents dry photographic plates

In the late nineteenth century, an eager U.S. photographer named George Eastman made breakthroughs that made it cheap and simple for anybody—not just professional photographers—to take photographs.

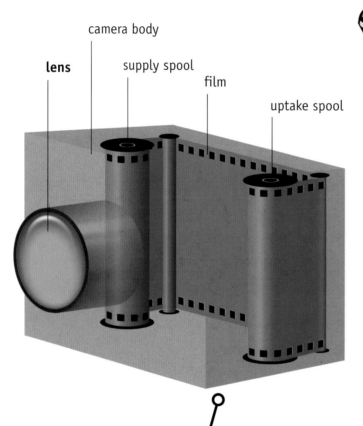

camera body

lens

supply spool

film

uptake spool

This diagram shows how roll film fits inside a camera.

EUREKA!

George Eastman spent years trying to make dry (instead of wet) photographic **plates** using a material called gelatin to hold the **light-sensitive** materials. He eventually succeeded, but soon realized that there was no future in the heavy and inconvenient glass plates. In 1884 he had the idea of putting the gelatin on a roll of paper instead. Professional photographers continued using plates, but paper roll **film** made small, cheap, and simple cameras possible.

12

1878—Eadweard Muybridge takes photographs of a galloping horse

1879—Muybridge invents the **zoopraxiscope**

1880—George Eastman begins selling dry plates for cameras

1885—Eastman begins to sell paper roll film

1875

1880

1885

George Eastman *(1854–1932)*

George Eastman began to take an interest in photography when, at the age of 24, he bought a "wet-plate" camera and photographic equipment to record his vacations. In 1880 he started the Eastman Dry Plate Company to produce dry photographic plates for cameras. In 1885 he developed paper roll film, then in 1888, the first Kodak camera. The camera was loaded with film for 100 photographs. It was an almost instant success. Eastman said his aim was "to make the camera as convenient as the pencil."

13

1887—Hannibal Goodwin makes the first **celluloid** sheet

1888—Eastman begins selling his first camera, called the Kodak. Thomas Edison invents the kinetoscope.

1892—The Eastman-Kodak company is formed

1890

1895

Paper roll film

By 1888 Eastman was selling simple box cameras. At the front was a **lens** and a **shutter**. When the shutter button was pressed, the shutter opened briefly to let light into the camera. The **image** was recorded on paper **film**. After a photograph was taken, the roll of film was wound so that a fresh piece of film was in place for the next photograph. Almost all cameras used roll film for the next 100 years.

When a roll of film was used up, the camera owner could send it to Eastman's company, Eastman-Kodak. The company **developed** the film and sent printed photographs back. Eastman invented a famous advertising slogan for this camera system: "You press the button, we do the rest."

The Kodak Camera

"*You press the button,*
we do the rest."

OR YOU CAN DO IT YOURSELF.

The only camera that anybody can use without instructions. As convenient to carry as an ordinary field glass   World-wide success.

The Kodak is for sale by all Photo stock dealers.
Send for the Primer, free.

The Eastman Dry Plate & Film Co.

Price, $25.00 — Loaded for 100 Pictures.   ROCHESTER, N. Y.
Re-loading, $2.00.

This is an advertisement for Eastman's first Kodak camera.

14

Celluloid film

The next advance in camera technology came with the invention of a new material called **celluloid**. It was first invented in the 1850s, but became popular in the 1860s, when it was used to make pool balls. George Eastman recognized that thin sheets of celluloid would be perfect for making photographic film. In 1889 he began making roll film from celluloid with a coating of **light-sensitive** gelatin.

The Box Brownie

In 1900 Eastman released a new model of camera that used celluloid film. This was the Box Brownie. The first Brownie was a simple box made out of wood and cardboard. It cost just $1 and was easy to use. The Brownie became one of the most popular cameras ever, and versions of it were made for another 60 years.

This is a 1902 Kodak Brownie camera with its packaging.

Setbacks

Celluloid was an extremely useful material, but it had a drawback—it was extremely flammable. It could easily burst into flames.

1913—The first 35-mm camera is introduced

PHOTOGRAPHING MOVEMENT

The moving pictures we see on television, computer screens, and movie screens are made up of many still **images** shown one after the other. Because our eyes remember an image for a brief moment, our brains are fooled into seeing a moving picture. This effect is called "persistence of vision." In the first half of the nineteenth century, **optical** toys such as the flip book made use of persistence of vision.

This picture from 1882 shows a **praxinoscope** projecting animated images on a screen.

To record a moving scene, such as a person running, we have to take photographs quickly one after the other. When these photographs are viewed as a fast sequence, the viewer sees the moving scene. The first photographs of movement were taken to study how animals and people move. They were taken by British photographer Eadweard Muybridge, using a separate camera for each photograph in the sequence.

This sequence of photographs was taken by Eadweard Muybridge to study how horses move.

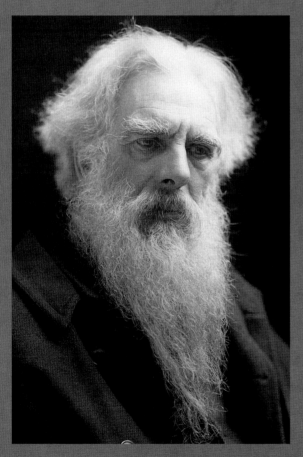

Eadweard Muybridge
(1830–1904)

Eadweard Muybridge was a pioneer of photographing movement. He began working as a bookseller, but later became a talented photographer of landscapes, especially of the American West. In the 1870s, Muybridge developed a way of using dozens of cameras to take a series of photographs of a galloping horse. He went on to photograph other animals and people in motion. He invented a device he called the **zoopraxiscope** to display the photographs as a moving image.

17

1927—Electric flashbulbs are invented

1935—Kodak produces Kodachrome, the first color **film**

Movies

Movie cameras became possible with the development of **celluloid** roll **film** by George Eastman (see page 15). To record a film, a movie camera had to take a photograph (called a **frame**) by opening and closing a **shutter**, then quickly move the film forward, ready to take another frame. It had to do this 20 or more times every second.

Thomas Edison built one of the first movie cameras. It used film that was 35 millimeters (mm), or 1.4 inches, wide with holes down each edge. It was made for him by Eastman-Kodak. A device inside the camera moved the film using the holes. Edison used a machine called a kinetoscope to show the films he recorded.

EUREKA!

In 1895 the French Lumière brothers opened the world's first movie theater in Paris. The film was projected onto a screen using a device they invented, called the cinematograph.

This is an early movie camera from 1896. It was called a cinematograph.

Thomas Edison *(1847–1931)*

The inventions of Thomas Edison changed the world forever. Edison set up a research laboratory where employees helped to develop his ideas. He made huge advances in the development of the electric lightbulb, and became famous in 1877 after his invention of the phonograph, the first ever sound-recording machine. In 1888 Edison invented the kinetoscope. He also invented one of the first movie cameras, which he called a kinetograph.

1948—Edwin Land perfects the Polaroid instant camera

1952—The first **endoscope** fitted with a camera is developed. It is called a gastrocamera.

1950

1955

CAMERA DEVELOPMENTS

Even in the 1990s, simple **film** cameras still worked in a very similar way to George Eastman's first Box Brownie, made nearly 100 years before. Like the Brownie, they used plastic roll film.

Film advances

In 1913 the first 35-mm camera was released. This used the same 35-mm film that had become popular in movie cameras. Soon 35 mm became the most common type of camera film. In 1935 Kodak introduced Kodachrome, the first color film. This was an exciting development. Before then, all films had been black and white.

This is a typical 35-mm camera from the 1930s.

EUREKA!

Edwin Land was a U.S. scientist and inventor. When his three-year-old daughter asked him why she could not see the photos he had taken right away, Land decided to make an instant camera. By 1948 he had perfected the Polaroid Land camera. It produced a paper photograph in just a few seconds.

Polaroid cameras make instant photographs, but the pictures can fade over time.

Flash

Photographers normally need bright light to illuminate their subjects. The first photographers worked in bright sunlight or used burning gunpowder to give off light. Electric flashbulbs were invented in 1927. They briefly lit up a scene, just as the photograph was taken.

Auto focusing

A camera must be **focused** so that the **image** from the **lens** falls right on the film, otherwise the photograph is blurry. It is focused by moving the lens closer to or further from the film. All cameras had to be focused by hand until 1978, when **autofocus** cameras were introduced.

21

DIGITAL CAMERAS

Nearly all modern cameras are digital cameras. A digital camera has an electronic sensor that records the **image** made by the **lens**. On the side of the sensor where the image falls, there are thousands of rows of tiny **light-sensitive** parts, called photosites. The camera measures the brightness and color of the image at each photosite. The camera then stores the information as numbers in its memory. The digital photograph is made up of millions of dots of color, called **pixels**.

This is the sensor chip from a digital camera. The image falls on the central, dark area.

A digital photograph is stored as a file in the camera's memory or on a disc. The file can be viewed on the camera's screen or transferred to a computer.

The first digital cameras were extremely expensive and only used in scientific instruments such as astronomical telescopes. However, by the early 1990s camera manufacturers introduced digital cameras that people could buy in stores, and they gradually became more common.

1978—Introduction of the first **autofocus** camera

It is simple to make your own movies with a modern digital video camera.

Video cameras

A video camera is a digital camera that records moving pictures. The camera takes 24 **frames** per second. The pictures are stored in the camera's memory or on a disc. Many digital cameras can also take short video clips.

Megapixels

Digital cameras take photographs that contain a certain number of pixels. The number is measured in units called megapixels. One megapixel is equal to one million pixels. The more pixels a photograph has, the more detail you can see. Early digital cameras had just one megapixel or less, but today, most cameras have 10 or 12 megapixels.

1991—The first digital camera is released

1992—Kodak introduces the Photo CD for storing digital photographs

THE IMPACT OF CAMERAS

Camera technology has changed dramatically since cameras were invented more than 150 years ago. In that time, photography has had a huge impact on the world. Photography began as a way to record people and events. Today, a lot of photography is still for that purpose, but it has dozens of other applications, too, including science, medicine, and security.

Science photography

In astronomy, cameras record **images** from telescopes on Earth's surface and onboard spacecraft. Some telescope cameras can record invisible rays such as infrared and X-rays, which tell us a great deal about the universe. Cameras on satellites also take images of Earth's surface. Other types of cameras record the images from microscopes. Scientists use high-speed video cameras that record hundreds or thousands of **frames** per second to study movement.

High-speed photo-finish cameras allow judges to look at close finishes in races.

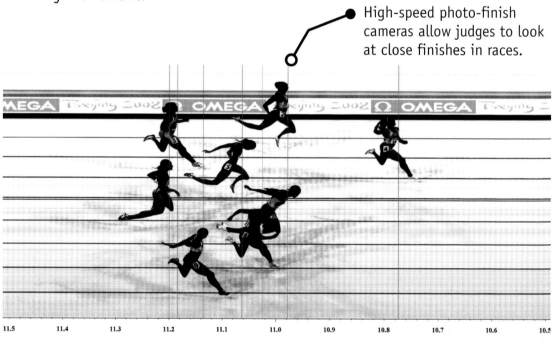

2000—The first camera phone is developed in Japan

Medical photography

Photography is used in medicine to investigate what is wrong with patients. X-ray photography can see through patients' bodies, to look for broken bones and other problems. An **endoscope** is a long tube with a camera at the end. It goes into a patient's body to allow a surgeon to see inside.

Capsule endoscopes such as this contain a tiny video camera that sees inside your body.

In 1895 German physicist Wilhelm Roentgen discovered X-rays when he noticed that rays were escaping from some experimental equipment. He soon discovered that X-rays pass through flesh but not bones. In 1896 doctors were using X-rays to diagnose illnesses.

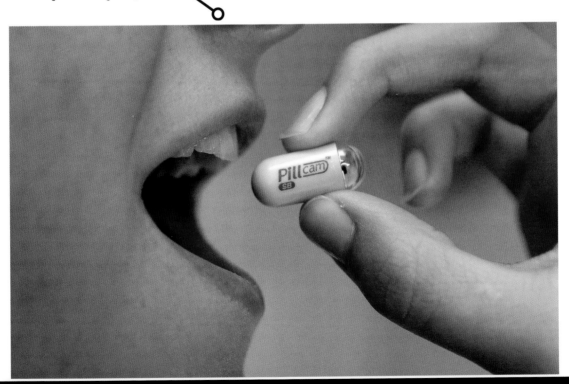

Famous photographs

Over the years since Louis Daguerre perfected his **daguerreotype** process, some photographs have become famous and are instantly recognizable to many people. One photograph recorded the terrible moment in 1937 when the airship *Hindenburg* burst into flames. The disaster killed 36 people. The photograph, taken by Murray Becker, was published in newspapers around the world. The airship industry lost the trust of its passengers and never really recovered.

This is Murray Becker's famous photograph of the *Hindenburg* airship crash.

Camera phones are a simple and handy way to take photographs.

Cameras everywhere

Over the decades since the camera was invented, photographers have taken countless photographs and filmmakers have made countless hours of film. They have recorded what the world and its people look like, as well as everyday events and world-changing moments.

Today, you can take a photograph with a digital camera by simply pressing a button, and it is almost as easy to make films using a digital video camera. We can even take photographs and videos with cell phones, with some MP3 players and other hand-held devices, and with webcams attached to computers.

It is also very easy for people to show the photographs they have taken to others by publishing their photographs and videos on the Internet. This has changed the way that major events are recorded, as passersby send their photographs and videos to television stations and newspapers.

TIMELINE

around 1000
The **camera obscura** is invented

around 1300
Eyeglass **lenses** are developed

around 1500
Camera obscuras start to be fitted with lenses

1851
Frederick Scott Archer invents the collodion process

1840
William Fox Talbot invents the calotype process

1839
Daguerre announces his **daguerreotype** process

1860s
Mathew Brady photographs the Civil War

1871
Richard Maddox invents dry photographic **plates**

1878
Eadweard Muybridge takes photographs of a galloping horse

1895
Wilhelm Roentgen discovers X-rays

1895
The Lumière brothers open the first movie theater

1892
The Eastman-Kodak company is formed

1896
X-rays are first used in medicine

1900
Kodak introduces the Box Brownie

1913
The first 35-mm camera is introduced

2000
The first camera phone is developed in Japan

1992
Kodak introduces the Photo CD for storing digital photographs

1816
Joseph Niépce records his first photographs

1824
Niépce tries using **bitumen** to record photographs

1827
Niépce takes the first photograph that still survives today

1835
Daguerre discovers that **mercury develops** a photograph

1834
The **zoetrope** shows moving **images** inside a spinning drum

1829
Niépce begins working with Louis Daguerre

1879
Eadweard Muybridge invents the **zoopraxiscope**

1880
George Eastman begins selling dry plates for cameras

1885
Eastman begins to sell paper roll **film**

1888
Eastman begins selling his first camera, called the Kodak

1888
Thomas Edison invents the kinetoscope

1887
Hannibal Goodwin makes the first **celluloid** sheet

1927
Electric flashbulbs are invented

1935
Kodak produces Kodachrome, the first color film

1948
Edwin Land perfects the Polaroid instant camera

1991
The first digital camera is released

1978
Introduction of the first **autofocus** camera

1952
The first **endoscope** fitted with a camera is developed. It is called a gastrocamera.

GLOSSARY

autofocus when a camera can automatically focus an image for you

bitumen black, tar-like material found in the ground

camera obscura camera that creates images but does not record them

celluloid early form of plastic

daguerreotype type of photographic process invented by Louis Daguerre, popular in the mid-1800s

develop make a photograph appear on film that has been exposed to light in a camera

endoscope medical instrument used to look inside the body

film thin sheet of plastic coated with light-sensitive material. Early film was made of paper, then later celluloid.

focus make a clear image of a scene fall on a camera's film or light sensor

frame single picture in a series. Movie cameras record a series of frames that together make up the movie.

image picture made by focusing the light rays from a scene onto a flat screen

lens disc of glass with curved surfaces that bend light rays as they pass through it

light-sensitive sensing or reacting to light. Photographic film is light-sensitive.

mercury silver-colored metal that is a liquid at room temperature

negative photograph in which the dark areas of the scene appear light, and light areas appear dark

optical to do with the eyes or seeing

pension regular payment made to people after they have stopped working

pixel dot of color on a photograph. Millions of pixels together make up an image.

plate sheet of metal or glass coated in light-sensitive chemicals

praxinoscope improved type of zoetrope that allows the moving image to be shown on a screen so that a group of people can watch it at the same time

salt substance made up of a metal combined with one or more type of non-metal, such as silver nitrate and sodium chloride

shutter part of a camera between the lens and the film or light sensor that opens briefly to let light coming through the lens hit the film or sensor

vapor gas formed when a liquid evaporates into the air

zoetrope early optical toy that has a series of drawings on the inside of a spinning cylinder. When a person looks through slits on the side of the cylinder, the picture inside looks as though it is moving.

zoopraxiscope machine like a zoetrope that projected a series of pictures painted on glass discs onto a screen so that they looked like they were moving. Later, the zoopraxiscope was used to show a series of photographs.

FIND OUT MORE

Books

Fandel, Jennifer. *Inventions and Discovery: George Eastman and the Kodak Camera*. North Mankato, Minn.: Capstone, 2007.

Jenner, Caryn. *Thomas Edison: The Great Inventor*. New York: Dorling Kindersley, 2007.

Raum, Elizabeth. *Inventions That Changed the World: The History of the Camera*. Chicago: Heinemann Library, 2008.

Websites

Visit the Daguerreian Society website and discover more about daguerreotypes:
www.daguerre.org

This website contains a history of Kodak and the work of George Eastman. Follow links to "About Kodak," then "Our Company," then "History of Kodak" at:
www.kodak.com

Watch some of Eadweard Muybridge's animations at:
www.artsmia.org/animal-locomotion

Places to visit

George Eastman House
900 East Avenue
Rochester, New York 14607
www.eastmanhouse.org

International Center of Photography
1133 Avenue of the Americas at 43rd Street
New York, New York 10036
www.icp.org

INDEX